PIANO · VOCAL · GUITAR

Billboard® SHEET MUSIC HITS 2000-2010

PLAY YOUR FAVORITE SONGS!

Produced by
Alfred Music Publishing Co., Inc.
P.O. Box 10003
Van Nuys, CA 91410-0003
alfred.com

Printed in USA.

ISBN-10: 0-7390-6968-3
ISBN-13: 978-0-7390-6968-4

 Alfred Cares. Contents printed on 100% recycled paper.

21 GUNS

Lyrics by
BILLIE JOE

Music by
GREEN DAY

Moderately slow ♩ = 84

Verses 1 & 3:

1. Do you know what's worth fight - ing for,_____
3. When you're at the_____ end of the road,_____

when it's not worth dy - ing for?_____
and you lost all sense of con - trol,_____

Does it take your breath_____ a - way_____ and you feel_____
and your thoughts your have tak - en their toll,_____ when your mind_

Verses 2 & 4:

2. Does the pain weigh out the pride?
4. Your faith walks on bro - ken glass,

And you look for a place to hide?
and the hang - o - ver does - n't pass.

Did some - one break your
Noth - ing's ev - er

heart in - side? You're in ru - ins.
built to last, you're in ru - ins.

4

6

Verse 5:

5. When it's time to___ live and let die,___ and you can't get an -

8

in - to the sky.＿＿＿ One, twen - ty - one guns,＿
(Ah.＿＿＿＿＿＿＿＿＿)

lay down your arms,＿ give up the fight.＿
(Ah.＿＿＿＿＿＿＿＿＿)

One, twen - ty - one guns,＿ throw up your arms＿ in - to the sky,＿
(Ah.

you and I.＿
(Ah.＿＿＿＿＿＿＿＿＿)

AIRPLANES

Words and Music by
JUSTIN FRANKS, TIM SOMMERS,
JEREMY DUSSOLLIET, BOBBY RAY SIMMONS
and ALEX GRANT

Airplanes - 6 - 1

14

Verse 2 (rap):
Somebody take me back to the days
Before this was a job, before I got paid,
Before it ever mattered what I had in my bank.
Yeah, back when I was tryin' to get a tip at Subway,
And back when I was rappin' for the hell of it.
But now-a-days, we rappin' to stay relevant.
I'm guessin' that if we can make some wishes outta airplanes,
Then maybe, yo, maybe I'll go back to the days
Before the politics that we call the rap game,
And back when ain't nobody listened to my mix tape,
And back before I tried to cover up my slang.
But this is for Decatur, what's up, Bobby Ray?
So can I get a wish to end the politics
And get back to the music that started this sh**?
So here I stand, and then again I say,
I'm hopin' we can make some wishes outta airplanes.
(To Chorus:)

APOLOGIZE

Words and Music by
RYAN TEDDER

Moderately slow, in 2 ♩ = 60

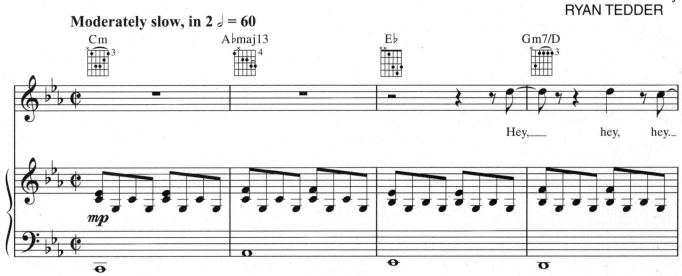

Hey,___ hey, hey.___

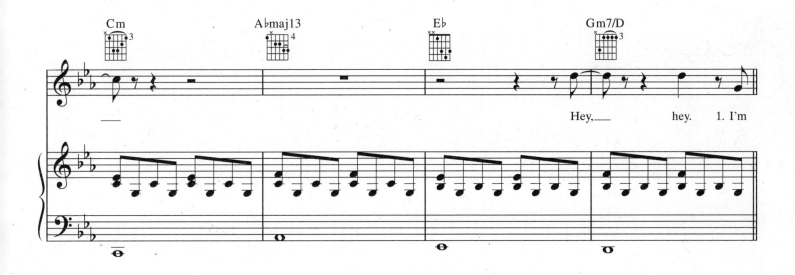

Hey,___ hey. 1. I'm

Verse 1:

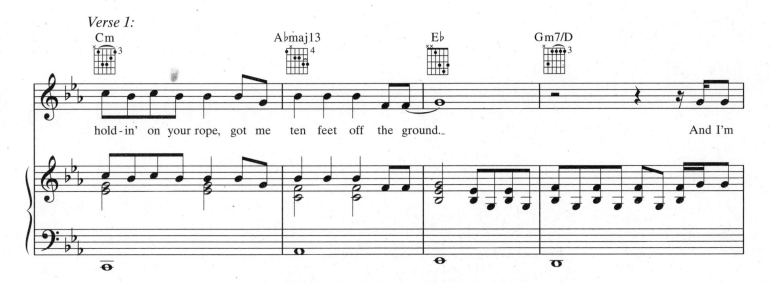

hold-in' on your rope, got me ten feet off the ground.___ And I'm

18

20

BAD DAY

Gtr. tuned down 1/2 step:
⑥ = E♭   ③ = G♭
⑤ = A♭   ② = B♭
④ = D♭   ① = E♭

Words and Music by
DANIEL POWTER

Bad Day - 8 - 1

Bridge 2:

BE WITHOUT YOU

Words and Music by
BRYAN MICHAEL COX, JOHNTA AUSTIN,
MARY J. BLIGE, and JASON PERRY

1. Chem-is-try was cra-zy from the get-go, nei-ther one of us knew why.
2. *See additional lyrics*

Be Without You - 6 - 1

Bridge:

See, this is real__ talk, c - 'mon, al - ways__ stay,_____ (no mat - ter what,) good or bad,__ (thick or thin,) right or wrong (all day, ev - 'ry day._____) Now if you're down on love or don't be - lieve,__ this ain't for you. And if you got it (No,__ this ain't__ for you._____)

deep in your heart, and deep down you know__ that it's true,_____ well, let me see you put your C - 'mon,__ c - 'mon,__ c - 'mon.__

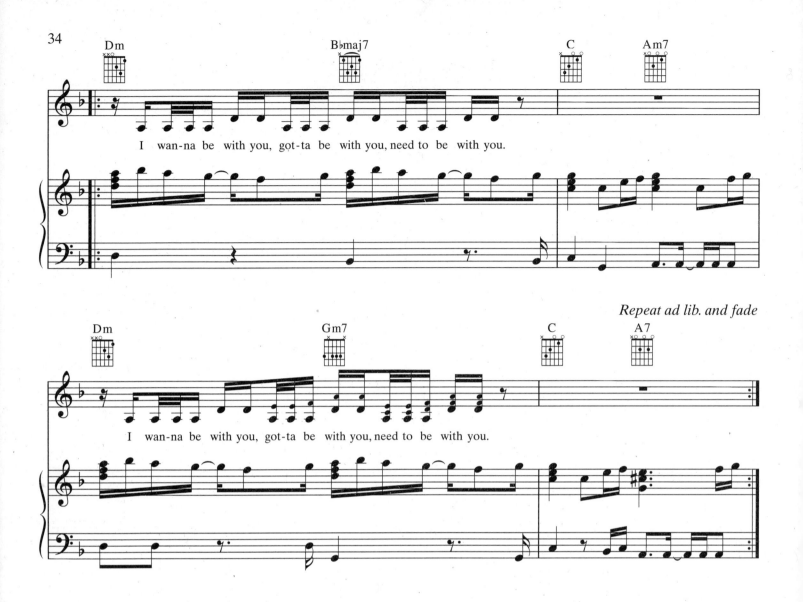

I wan-na be with you, got-ta be with you, need to be with you.

Repeat ad lib. and fade

I wan-na be with you, got-ta be with you, need to be with you.

Verse 2:
I've got a question for you,
(See, I already know the answer.)
Still, I wanna ask you:
Would you lie? *(no)*
Make me cry? *(no)*
Do somethin' behind my back and then try to cover it up?
Well, neither would I, baby.
My love is only your love, *(yes)*
I'll always be faithful. *(yes)*
I'm for real *(yes)*
And with us you'll always know the deal.
(To Chorus:)

BREAKAWAY

Words and Music by
MATTHEW GERRARD, BRIDGET BENENATE
and AVRIL LAVIGNE

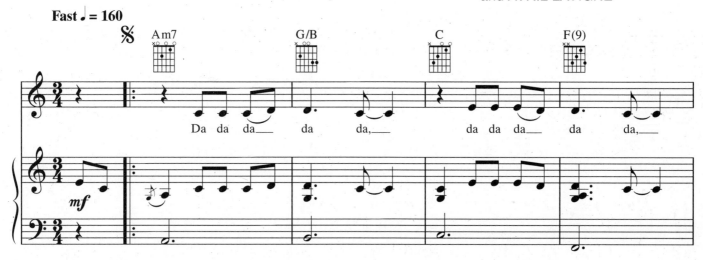

Da da da___ da da,___ da da da___ da da,___

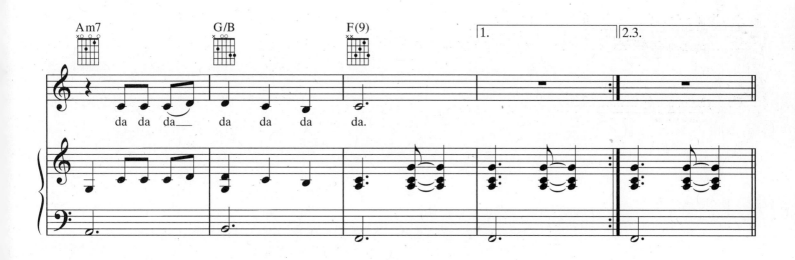

da da da___ da da da da.

Verse:

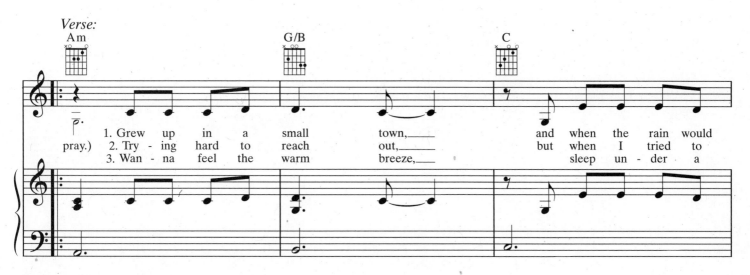

1. Grew up in a small town,___ and when the rain would
pray.) 2. Try - ing hard to reach out,___ but when I tried to
3. Wan - na feel the warm breeze,___ sleep un - der a

36

38

Breakaway - 5 - 4

COMPLICATED

Gtr. tuned down 1 whole step:
⑥ = D ③ = F
⑤ = G ② = A
④ = C ① = D

Words and Music by
LAUREN CHRISTY, GRAHAM EDWARDS,
SCOTT SPOCK and AVRIL LAVIGNE

Moderately slow rock ♩ = 80

Verse:

1. Chill out, what-cha yell - ing for? Lay back, it's all been done___ be - fore.
2. You come o - ver, un - an - nounced, dressed up___ like you're some - thing else.
   no. 3. *(Inst. solo ad lib....)*

Complicated - 4 - 1

Complicated - 4 - 2

CRAZY

Words and Music by
THOMAS DECARLO CALLAWAY, BRIAN JOSEPH BURTON,
GIANFRANCO REVERBERI and GIAN PIERO REVERBERI

Crazy - 5 - 1

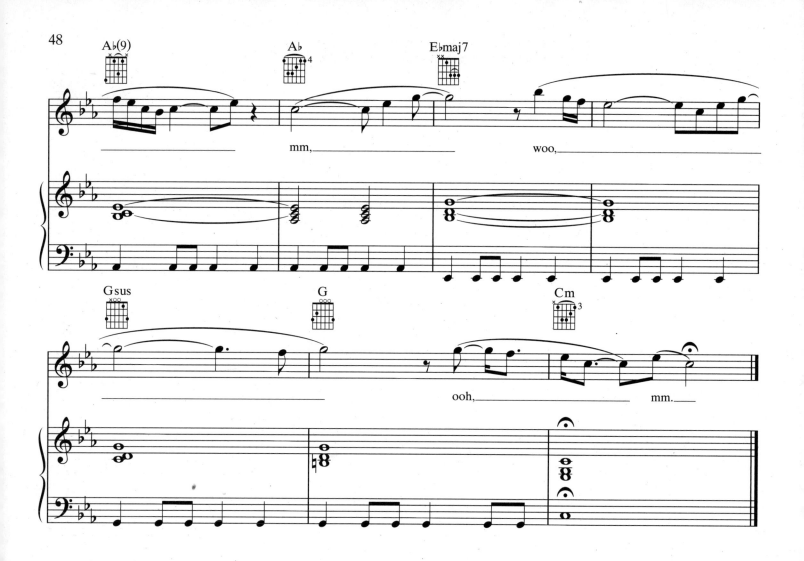

Verse 2:
Come on now, who do you, who do you,
Who do you, who do you think you are?
Ha ha ha, bless your soul,
You really think you're in control.

Chorus 2:
Well, I think you're crazy.
I think you're crazy.
I think you're crazy,
Just like me.
My heroes had the heart to lose their lives out on a limb,
And all I remember is thinking I want to be like them.

Verse 3:
Ever since I was little, ever since I was little it looked like fun.
And it's no coincidence I've come,
And I can die when I'm done.

Chorus 3:
But maybe I'm crazy.
Maybe you're crazy.
Maybe we're crazy.
Probably.
(To Coda)

HANGING BY A MOMENT

Words and Music by
JASON WADE

Gtr. tuned down 1/2 step,
"Drop D" tuning:
⑥ = Db   ③ = Gb
⑤ = Ab   ② = Bb
④ = Db   ① = Eb

Moderately ♩ = 126

Guitar → D5

Piano → Db5

mp

Verse 1:

1. Des - p'rate_ for chang - ing._

Starv - ing_ for_ truth._ I'm clos - er to where I start-

ed._ I'm chas - ing af - ter you._ I'm fall - ing e - ven

Hanging by a Moment - 7 - 1

50

Verse 3:

3. Des - p'rate_ for chang - ing._____ Starv - ing__ for__ truth.__

__ I'm clos - er to where I start - ed._____ I'm

FALLING SLOWLY

Words and Music by
GLEN HANSARD and
MARKETA IRGLOVA

Slowly ♩ = 69

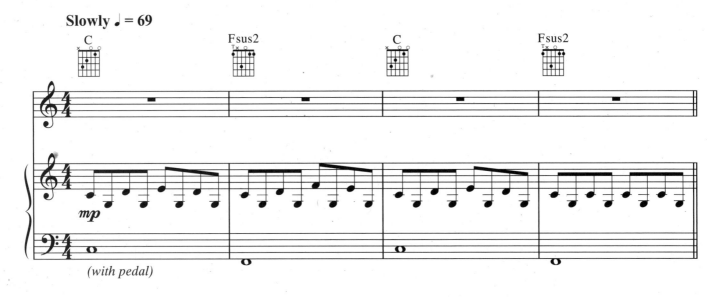

(with pedal)

Verse 1:

1. I don't know you, but I want you all the more for that.

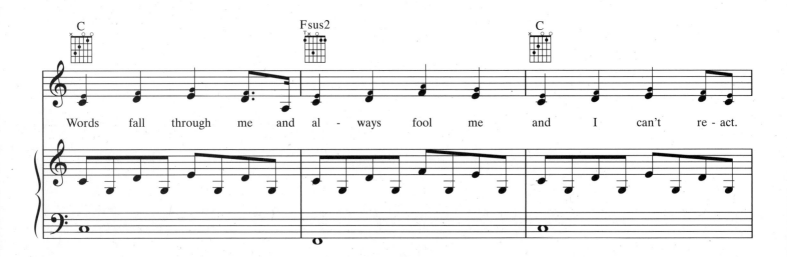

Words fall through me and al-ways fool me and I can't re-act.

Falling Slowly - 6 - 1

Falling Slowly - 6 - 2

58

Verse 2:

HAVEN'T MET YOU YET

Words and Music by
MICHAEL BUBLÉ, ALAN CHANG
and AMY FOSTER

Haven't Met You Yet - 8 - 1

HOME

Words and Music by
MICHAEL BUBLÉ, ALAN CHANG
and AMY FOSTER

1. An-oth-er sum-mer day has come and gone a-way in Par-is and Rome,_ but I wan-na go home._

May be sur-round-ed by a mil-lion peo-ple, I still feel all a - lone,_ just wan-na go home._

Oh, I miss you, you know. I've been

keep-ing all_ the let-ters_ that I wrote to you, each one a line_
feel just like_ I'm liv-ing_ some-one els - e's life. It's like I just stepped_

or two,___ "I'm fine, ba - by. How are you?"___ Well, I would
out - side,___ when ev-'ry-thing was go - ing right.___ And I

send them, but___ I know___ that it's___ just not e-nough. My words were cold___
know just why___ you could - n't come___ a - long with me. This was not___

___ and flat,___ and you de-serve more_____ than that.
___ your dream,_ but you al - ways be - lieved_____ in me.

An-oth-er ae-ro-plane, an-oth-er sun-ny place._ I'm luck-y, I know,___ but I wan-na go home.
An-oth-er win-ter day has come and gone a-way in ei-ther Par-is or Rome,_ and I wan-na go home._

74

And I

⊕ Coda

home.___ And I'm sur-round-ed by a mil-lion peo-ple, I,

I still feel a-lone,___ oh, let___ me go home.___ Oh, I miss you, you

Chorus:

know. Let me go home.___

HOT N COLD

Words and Music by
KATY PERRY, LUKASZ GOTTWALD
and MAX MARTIN

Hot n Cold - 6 - 1

78

Am · C · G · D
— we break up. We kiss,— we make up.— (You.— You don't real - ly wan - na

Am · C
stay, no.— (You.— But you don't real - ly wan - na go - o.— You're hot,—

G · D · Am · C
— then you're cold. You're yes,— then you're no. You're in,— then you're out. You're up,—

1.
N.C.
— then you're down.—

mp

Hot n Cold - 6 - 3

79

Hot n Cold - 6 - 4

HOW TO SAVE A LIFE

Gtr. tuned down 1 whole step:
⑥ = D   ③ = F
⑤ = G   ② = A
④ = C   ① = D

Words and Music by
JOSEPH KING and
ISAAC SLADE

How to Save a Life - 6 - 1

HEY THERE DELILAH

Words and Music by
TOM HIGGENSON

Moderately ♩ = 108

Verses 1 & 2:

1. Hey there, De - li - lah, what's it like in New York Cit - y? I'm a thou-
2. Hey there, De - li - lah, I know times are get - ting hard, but just be - lieve

sand miles a - way, but, girl, to - night you look so pret - ty, yes, you do.
me, girl, some - day I'll pay the bills with this gui - tar, we'll have it good.

Bridge:

thou-sand miles_ seems pret-ty far,__ but they've_ got planes_ and trains_ and cars.__ I'd walk_

__ to you__ if I had no oth-er way.__ Our

friends would all__ make fun of us,__ and we'll__ just laugh_ a-long_ be-cause_ we know_

__ that none of them__ have felt__ this way. De-

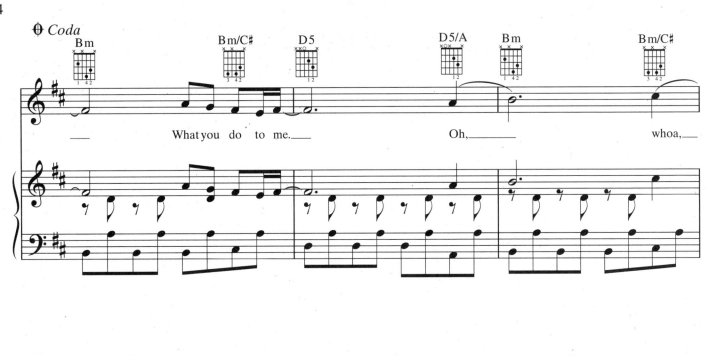

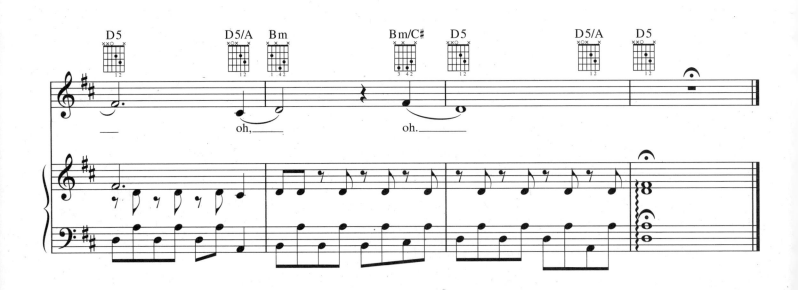

MY IMMORTAL

Words and Music by
BEN MOODY, AMY LEE
and DAVID HODGES

Slowly and freely ♩ = 80

Verse:

1. I'm so tired of be - ing here,___ sup - pressed___ by all___ my
2. *See additional lyrics*

child - ish fears._____ And if you have to leave,___

My Immortal - 5 - 1

98

My Immortal - 5 - 4

Verse 2:
You used to captivate me
By your resonating light.
But, now I'm bound by the life you left behind.
Your face, it haunts
My once pleasant dreams.
Your voice, it chased away
All the sanity in me.
These wounds won't seem to heal.
This pain is just too real.
There's just too much that time can not erase.
(To Chorus:)

I'M YOURS

Words and Music by
JASON MRAZ

*Original recording in key of B.

fell right through the cracks.___ Now I'm try-in' to get___ back._____ Be-fore the

cool done run out, I'll be giv-in' it my best-est, and noth-in's gon-na stop me but di-vine in-ter-ven-tion. I

reck-on it's a-gain my turn___ to___ win some___ or lose___ some. But

Chorus:

I___ won't hes-i-tate no more,___ no___ more.___ It can-not

105

I'm Yours - 8 - 6

LOVE STORY

Words and Music by
TAYLOR SWIFT

Chorus:

NEW SOUL

Words and Music by
YAEL NAIM and DAVID DONATIEN

Chorus:

118

New Soul - 6 - 3

Verse 3:

This is a hap - py end._ Come and give me your hand.

I'll take you far___ a - way.___ 3. I'm a new soul, I came to this

strange world hop - ing I could learn a bit 'bout how to give and take._ But since I

came here, felt the joy and the fear, find - ing my - self mak - ing ev - 'ry pos - si - ble mis -

PHOTOGRAPH

Gtr. tuned down 1/2 step:
⑥ = E♭   ③ = G♭
⑤ = A♭   ② = B♭
④ = D♭   ① = E♭

Lyrics by
CHAD KROEGER

Music by
NICKELBACK

126

Photograph - 6 - 5

TEMPORARY HOME

Words and Music by
CARRIE UNDERWOOD, LUKE LAIRD
and ZAC MALOY

Temporary Home - 6 - 1

NEED YOU NOW

Words and Music by
DAVE HAYWOOD, CHARLES KELLEY,
HILLARY SCOTT and JOSH KEAR

*Alternate between open G and A on the 3rd string.

Need You Now - 7 - 1

138

Need You Now - 7 - 5

UMBRELLA

Words and Music by
TERIUS NASH, SHAWN CARTER,
THADDIS HARRELL and
CHRISTOPHER STEWART

Umbrella - 7 - 1

142

144

Umbrella - 7 - 4

WE ARE THE WORLD 25 FOR HAITI

Words and Music by
MICHAEL JACKSON and LIONEL RICHIE

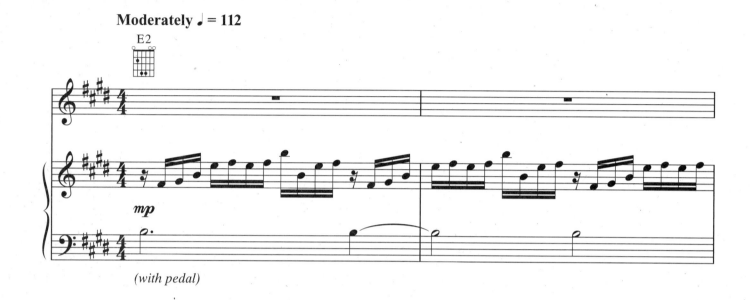

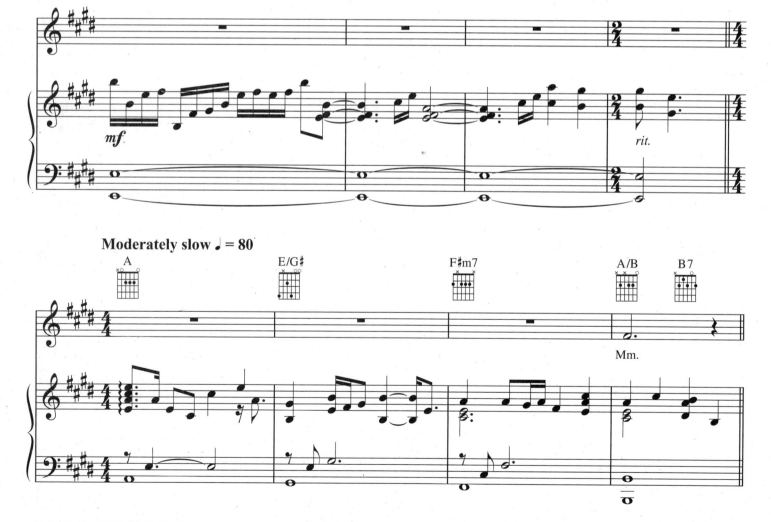

We Are the World 25 for Haiti - 12 - 1

153

We Are the World 25 for Haiti - 12 - 6

156

158

We Are the World 25 for Haiti - 12 - 11

Rap:
We all need somebody that we can lean on,
When you wake up, look around and see that your dream's gone.
When the earth quakes, we'll help you make it through the storm,
When the floor breaks, a magic carpet to stand on.
We are the world, united by love so strong,
When the radio isn't on, you can hear the song.
A guided light on the dark road you're walking on,
A sign post to find the dreams you thought was gone.
Someone to help you move the obstacles you stumbled on,
Someone to help you rebuild after the rubble's gone.
We are the world, connected by a common bond,
Love, the whole planet singing along.
(To Chorus:)

WE BELONG TOGETHER

Words and Music by
KENNETH EDMONDS, DARNELL BRISTOL, SIDNEY JOHNSON,
JOHNTA AUSTIN, JERMAINE DUPRI, MANUEL SEAL, SANDRA SULLY,
MARIAH CAREY, PATRICK MOTEN and BOBBY WOMACK

We Belong Together - 7 - 1

Verse 1:

1. I did-n't mean it when I said I did-n't love you so. I should have held on tight, I nev-er should have let you go.

I did-n't know noth-ing, I was stu-pid, I was fool-ish, I was ly-in' to my-self._____

I could-n't have fath-omed I would ev-er be with-out your love. Nev-er i-mag-ined I'd be sit-ting here be-side my-self.

Guess I did-n't know you, 'cause I did-n't know me, but I thought I knew ev-'ry-thing. I nev-er felt_____

162

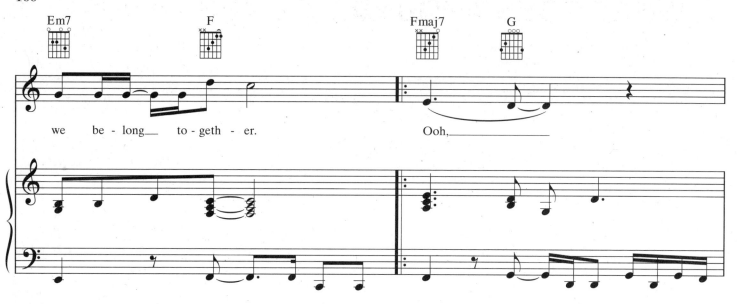

WHAT GOES AROUND... COMES AROUND

Words and Music by
TIM MOSLEY, NATE HILLS
and JUSTIN TIMBERLAKE

What Goes Around... Comes Around - 7 - 1

WHEN I LOOK AT YOU

Words and Music by
HILLARY LINDSEY and JOHN SHANKS

Slowly ♩. = 46

Verse 1 (sing 1st time only):

1. Ev-'ry-bod-y needs in-spi-ra-tion, ev-'ry-bod-y needs

Verse 2 (sing 2nd time only):

(2.) look at you I see for-give-ness. I see

a song, a beau-ti-ful mel-o-dy

the truth. You love me for who I am,

*Original recording in F# major.

when the night's_____ so long._____ 'Cause there is no_____

like the stars hold_____ the moon_____ right there where

_____ guar-an - tee_____ that this life is eas - y._____ Yeah, when_

they be - long,_____ and I know I'm not a - lone._____ Yeah, when_

Chorus:

my_____ world is fall - ing a - part,_ when there's no_____ light to break_

178

WITH ARMS WIDE OPEN

Words and Music by
MARK TREMONTI
and SCOTT STAPP

With Arms Wide Open - 8 - 1

YOU RAISE ME UP

Words and Music by
ROLF LOVLAND and
BRENDAN GRAHAM

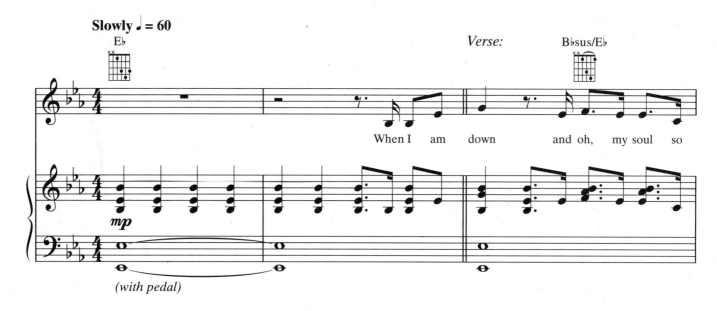

When I am down and oh, my soul so

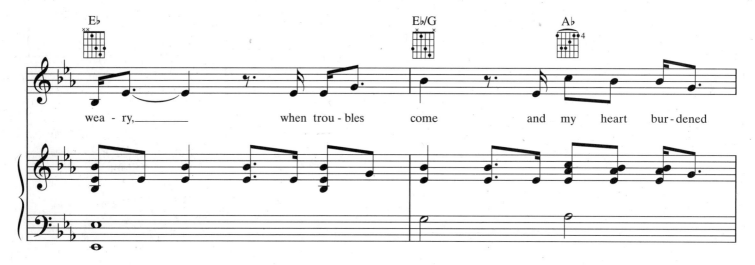

wea - ry,_____ when trou - bles come and my heart bur - dened

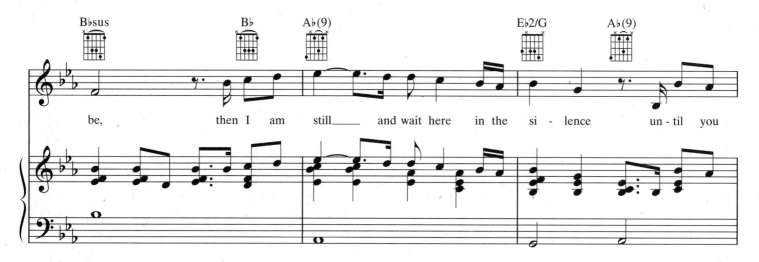

be, then I am still____ and wait here in the si - lence un - til you

You Raise Me Up - 5 - 1

192

You Raise Me Up - 5 - 5